Ancestry Unfinished
Poems of a Lost Generation

To Lisa — for being there from the beginning; to every good and beautiful journey.

Ancestry Unfinished
Poems of a Lost Generation

by

Yasmin Mariam Kloth

Cover design by Shay Culligan
Cover photograph by Yasmin Mariam Kloth

ISBN: 978-1-63980-174-9

Kelsay Books
502 South 1040 East, A-119
American Fork, Utah 84003
Kelsaybooks.com

*For Mado and Moomy,
my grandmothers.*

*In memory of Mona Latif-Ghattas,
my godmother, my aunt.*

Acknowledgments

I am grateful to the following journals, in which some of the poems in this book have been previously published. A few of them may be in a slightly modified form.

All the Sins: "Feather"

Bravery Magazine: "Little Things"

Cathexis Northwest Press: "Jasmine Flower"

Chestnut Review: "Here"

Flock: "I've Named These Ashes"

JuxtaProse Magazine: "Cell Division and Other Science," "Small Thing"

Kairos Literary Journal: "Silver-Plated"

Open: Journal of Arts & Letters: "At the Souk"

Rockvale Review: "Bones," "Bird's Tongue"

The Tiger Moth Review: "Source," "Banyan Song" ("Banyan Song" received the third-place award for the 2021 Hawker Prize for Southeast Asian Poetry)

The Voices Project: "Notice You"

Willawaw Journal: "Ritual"

With Gratitude

This poetry collection began at a week-long poetry writer's workshop at Kenyon College in the summer of 2019. Each daily poetry prompt brought a new reflection on my family's Middle Eastern heritage. I'm deeply grateful to all the talented writers in my cohort who gave me the space to explore these parts of my story and who were kind and direct in their critiques. To Amanda Gunn, who quietly taught me how to follow my heart. And to Natalie Shapero our teacher, who taught us how to approach each other's words without judgment; how to ask questions of the poetry in front of us.

I am also grateful to the Black Dog Poetry community based in Nashville, Tennessee, a community I would never have been a part of had they not gone virtual during the pandemic. This group of exceptional writers is an inspiration, each writer with their own unique voice and story. Many thanks to Nancy Posey and Sandy Coomer, who run the monthly sessions and who have given poets across the country a shared space to have their voices heard.

To Shahé Mankerian, whose poetry treads the impossible line between hard and soft, he has shown me new layers of the Middle East.

To the editors at Kelsay Books who believed in this little book, thank you. To all the people in my orbit who have supported my writing from the beginning, your encouragement has kept me tethered to my dreams. If I were to write all your names down, I would surely miss someone, so please know I'm talking to you.

To my dad, who has always believed that I can do anything, and to my mom, who had so much still to do, I know she sees this; she is the soul of this book.

And to G and E, my loves, without whom none of these words would ever be written.

Contents

Grandmothers

Ritual

My grandmother reads
coffee grounds with two hands
she holds blue and red flowers
of the Turkish coffee cup. First, she
presses the saucer against
the ceramic lip and the sound
of hard surfaces rings
through the room. She
flips the two together
for a moment they are dancing
to her hum. My grandmother hums
a low murmur like a chant
to what's left of the liquid,
hums to a pool of silk.
The grounds hold tight
to the walls of the cup
and the shapes tell stories
I will never understand.

I am thirteen and old enough
now to hear my grandmother
read my mother's cup.
It takes time. They drink
the coffee first with their backs
in chairs my grandmother
embroidered, gifts she gave
when my parents married
and they talk about their lives,
this time that has passed.
They talk about place and
the space that fills the distance
to there.

My grandmother holds
my mother's cup in her hands.
She goes to speak.
We wait in the silence
of her pause

and her drifting gaze.

In Shade and Sun

When I lose a word here,
or there, I worry
I'll inherit her dementia.
It's like the macular
degeneration that took
her eyesight,
and the doctors say
could manifest
in my father's eyes,
and maybe mine.

She couldn't remember
who I was the last time
we spoke on the phone—
chirped "Who? Who?"
like a bird, like a child
lost in a crowd.
I sucked my words
through the cave
of my throat, let 2,000 miles
of road and mountain
spread between us
like a river in the rain.

Is all loss a line?
Her loss is an ocean.
When I was a child
she kept chocolate wafers
in her cupboard in Cairo
and glass bottles of Pepsi
in the fridge. Apartments
couldn't keep the afternoon heat
in winter, and she'd wrap
a hot water bottle beneath

my sheets, wrap my body
as if I had been laying
in the sun.

Now, the California sun
spreads across the shade
of her eyes. When she turns
her face to a place in the sky,
I don't know what light
may flicker in spots or waves.
I don't know if I'm still
a granddaughter.

I don't know if Cairo exists.

Funny Thing

I am forgetting everyday words,
the ones in my daughter's vocabulary—
like goggles and backpack.

All my other senses seem to work.
Perhaps they are sharper still.
The smell of pine trees in late October,
brown needles like shredded knafeh spilled
on pavement. The sight of a young girl
in dog costume running on the neighbor's lawn,
her white tail chasing her body
until she disappears into the golden light
of her home. The sound of the wind
breaking the bones of the trees
on our quiet street.

Should I worry my words are escaping
my mind as if they've slithered their bodies
between cornstalks, between reeds?
You have this problem too, I know.
You spoke three languages once.
With time now, one.
You choose Arabic first, call me
by my mother's name, ask me
questions I don't understand. I'm worried
my face makes you miss her more.
The funny thing is—
I replace the gaps in my English
with the few Arabic words I know.
The funny thing is—
between the two of us,
we've remembered enough
to make us whole.

Hand Rolled Wisdom

My grandmother's grape leaves
are the only ones I'll eat.

She'll pull them like tissue paper
from an oily jar, take
her mottled hand to wild leaves
from vines, from trees, a plastic bag
of yellow veins crisp in the sun.

My grandmother's grape leaves
are made in many parts,
three days,
one night. The night
my mother died, a family friend
made Persian food we ate in silence
in a sterile room. There were no grape leaves,
but Tahdig, rice burned orange
burned turmeric and saffron
burned broken grains on my hospital plate.

My grandmother's grape leaves
are first washed, cut, dried, leaves
stretched wide on the counter
open mouths
            waiting to be stuffed.

My grandmother rolls her grape leaves by hand,
rolls grape leaves while watching *Days of our Lives,*
rolls grape leaves into thin bodies—
don't bulge or break.
She tolerates my time
in the kitchen, winces

when I over-, under-stuff, and holds
my hands in the way
she held my mother's that day.
That is to say: Gently.

My grandmother's grape leaves
are the only ones I'll eat.

Leaves from vines she picked the day before
wise to rain and time—
and our quiet lives.

Forty Days

No one warned you
your husband
would have trouble
where the tracks hit the sand.
No one warned
his car with its soft shell
and primitive gears
would kick forward
instead of back warned
the train would come pink
dust, deserted road.

You didn't want to know
the sound the metal made
when it broke, didn't want
the things retrieved didn't
want the weather, or
time of day.

You wore black for
forty days. Forty years
forward—

No one warned you
your daughter
her flipped cup
of Turkish grounds showed
shapes she read in secret.
No one warned
her line in the center
of her palm would break
in the middle warned
the train in winter
when the trees were bare.

No one warned you
the story of her sickness
what she concealed.
You measured
in strings of silence
the time she stole.

You wore black for
forty days.

You wear
black.

After the Cocktail Hour

It's after 5 o'clock in the afternoon.
The sun is slanting on the balcony
at an angle. It cuts a line on the tablecloth
and between my eyes.
She's had her scotch heavy on ice,
this amber liquid I measured with two fingers
into a crystal glass she brought with her
across an ocean when she left her country
those years ago.
I poured two more fingers for myself.

We've walked indoors from the wind.
She tells me I can have anything
in the spare bedroom after she dies.
It's full of my mother's photos and paintings,
an embroidered scene of a farm, girl, and cow.
I can't look too closely at the things she's gathered.
It's not the memory of my mother that hangs unspoken.
It's my grandmother's pain plastered to these walls
like a pause in a sentence.
Like a breath, a beat, a promise
bent in the middle.

Nothing has changed in this apartment over time.
Perhaps a thread from my grandmother's embroidery
has come undone.
Perhaps a cucumber in the fridge has gone bad. The tiny ones
she uses in her thick yogurt dip heavy on garlic and mint.
It's a tile that has cracked in the bathroom.
Or the perfume by her mirror that evaporated one drop
overnight.
I do not want to touch anything.
I do not want to cause change or movement.
I do not want to remember in the room
of all the reclaimed things.

I want for my grandmother peace
in these long, last, gray years.
To steady the hand that steadies the tilted frames
of the life she lost.

Banyan Song

My grandmother
made a home in the snow
when she knew nothing
of snow, transplanted from the shade
of Banyan trees.

In the years after
her husband died, her roots
grew low and dry.
She was easy to pluck
from her homeland, followed
children who'd already left
for new life.

I visited her there
in her apartment in Montreal.
Nothing had changed
in the years that expanded into spaces
an ocean's water could not fill.
My daughter hugged her in the entry
and she folded like a paper airplane
at the waist.
She had never been someone's
great-grandmother before.
This was too much love
for her heart to give.

The distance between
their generations is not age.
The distance is language and loss.
The distance is the root
of the Banyan tree, measured in meters
from its leaves to the earth.

My grandmother consumes
this knowledge
with a nose in my daughter's hair.

Ancestry Unfinished

You played the Oud in the evenings.
You took your place on the balcony,
adjusted the strings and your line of sight
with the Nile. This is what my aunt
tells me was your ritual.

I imagine you in many ways—
hands and face, a black and white
photograph, a pool of pigeons.
I'd stare, search
for parts of myself in the way
you held your mouth, search
for parts of myself in your stance.

Two of your big-bellied instruments remain.
One is in your apartment in Cairo.
My aunt repaired its body, tightened
its strings. Musicians can play it now
and when they do, old notes wake
as if they were hooks on a rising sun.

I have the other one.
I cannot hear its broken heart.
I was not born with hands to strings,
hands to keys, hands praised,
hands undone on tangled chords.

I imagine what it was for you
to play this once—search
for your fingerprints, wonder if I carry
the same concentric circles
on the soft pads of my fingers,
wonder how much of your ancestry
traveled with the wood
of your guitar.

I do not play your instrument.
I do not speak your language.
I do not smoke the pipe I know
you hooked in the corner of your mouth
and I imagine it smelled of roasted apples,
the way I imagine the smell of your skin;
the way I know my grandmother knew
the depth of every wrinkle
in your hands.

What has been lost across the ocean?
I am not prepared for the questions
my daughter will ask me, why
her middle name is unlike other names
of the kids in her class, why
the strange guitar in her home
is fat in the middle, why
the inlay in its center
looks like stained glass; why
the notes sound unfinished
and out of place, and will they

one day

be repaired?

A merry heart does good, like
medicine,
But a broken spirit dries the bones.
—Proverbs 17:22 (NKJV)

I've Named These Ashes

Each year the bones of my ancestors
turn more brittle and gray.
I think how so many must be buried
in the shade of cedar trees. Others, in reeds
by the Nile. I imagine skeletons
walking waves in the desert.
I imagine walking bone bodies
a line beneath the sun.

My grandfather's crypt is in Coptic Cairo.
There's a bust of his face (or is it his grandfather's face?)
at the door you do not enter.
Two decades have passed since I visited last.
My mother stood next to me
LATIF in sandstone letters
looking down at her.
She stared at her surname
as if she had never seen it before.
Her face turned red
and she turned away from me.

My mother was never buried.
Her ashes sit in a smooth wooden box
on a desk in my father's apartment in Ohio.
My grandmother paces her world quietly
someplace else. She wrings her hands.
She cannot visit my mother
so she builds a shrine in the spare room
between the TV and the daybed.

I visit my father, and I forget
my mother is there. Once,

I had a terrible fight with my brother
in earshot of her ashes.
We broke wide the gulf
of our fragile family.

LATIF in Arabic means gentle, kind.
Will I fail to know where I came from
if I let the ocean swallow more
of my country's coastline?
Will I forget the names
of those who made me if I do not
write them down?

It doesn't matter.
We are all ash.
When we mix with rain and sand,
we go back to the place
we were born.

The Port of Beirut

The reports say:
the force of the explosion
sucked the sea water in,
then out.
Did the blue sky, hot sun
know the red smoke
was a warning in the light?

I was born thousands
of miles away with feet
on American soil, my blood
sticky with generations
from somewhere over there.
Did I need a DNA test
to tell me these
are my people
in a border
by the sea?

Where am I from;   ·
Where do I go,
if the coastline
that made me
from salt and sand
is nothing—
is water and dust?

Everything that broke that day
broke in me—

sea and sky
sea and sky
sea and sky

and heart.

Mothers

Bones

I.

The panoramic dental x-ray
showed a section of my skeleton
smiling from my nose to my chin.
The hygienist explained
all the bones of my skull, tip of a Bic
to the screen. Concave and convex curves,
sinus cavities like dark lakes
in an open field. There were my teeth
neatly in a row, roots long and clean
living like tall pines on a hill,
nerve endings we don't think
to remember
until the hidden network
throbs in gentle waves.
I'm exposed to this stranger
in black and white film.
Can she tell if these bones
look like someone else's bones and
the names of all the people
who gave them to me?

II.

In the bath, my daughter looks
at me, her eyes level with the tub
so all I see are my eyes
looking back at me.
What line in my Syrian-Lebanese blood
made eyes the shape of delicate ovals
with points at either end?

The skin that covers my skeleton
knows much more about the sun,
my bones know the shape and color
of the earth. It was my mother's bones
that broke down first when cancer returned.
What line in her Syrian-Lebanese blood
sent her damaged cells?

III.

I touch the bones at the base of my eyes.
There are hard places here and soft.
Can the doctors tell me why and
the names of all the people
who made me easy to cry?
My bones tell me
I am already old inside my body.
What will I tell my daughter
when she asks me how
she was made?

Source

My parents grew up
on an island in the Nile.
On a map, it's the shape
of a vessel docked
in blue-green waters. On a map,
the Nile flows North, the shape
of a lotus flower, arms
opening out to sea.

I took a boat once
between Luxor and Aswan.
There is no modern city
in this stretch of water and land.
How can there be
in a place where the river is older
than pieces of the sky?
How can there be on these banks,
where homes are sand, trees
waiting for the wind?

I stood on the deck, watched old worlds
float by. Men on feluccas
in white cotton looked at me
with the whites of their eyes.
They were kings.
They gave me riches
with their smiles, their faces wrinkled
by the sun, valleys of skin
in the valley of the Nile.

My parents didn't raise me here.
They brought their language,
their food, their music,

their hopes for a family in luggage
unpacked in New York.
I would not understand
the source of what they left
for many years.

This is how I learned
how the felucca travels.
Light on water,
with a sail to the wind.

Bird's Tongue

I have a memory of my mother
in the kitchen cooking her *Shurbat Lisan Asfour*—
Bird's Tongue Soup, small
pasta grains like rice
like lean bodies laying
in the sand, laying
in a boiling broth.
From my place
in the room across the way
I could smell the lime
she squeezed into the liquid,
my small body protector
to a potted plant with pink buds.
I couldn't help myself, buds
too round and full and soft.
First one, just one from the stem
I told myself, plant rustling leaves
as I dropped its bud body
lightly in the soil.
Another.
Another.
Another.
I heard my mother call my name.
Another.
I heard her cross the room.
Another in the soil.
I saw her figure above me
like a shadow or a dream.
Her reprimand came in French first
then Arabic. She wanted answers
for my actions and her now naked
plant. How could I explain?

I wanted to know touch, hold
soft skin in my young hands, smell
salt from new soup roiling, loom
a dream high and bright
above another life.

Jasmine Flower

I never asked my mother
for the list she made
of other names
I could have been
the day I was born.
I knew the one she gave me
was the only one she loved,
name I bent into a boomerang
so it never quite sounded
like its Arabic origin, so
I could blend
in my American schools
the way a bird will press
brown feathers
against the grass, become
the grass even though
I hungered
for the way my family
pronounced my name,
the "s" in the middle long
and soft: a song, a lost note,
a scent I knew once
on my mother's skin,
leftover garlic and salt
leftovers
of the person I was.
My mother named me
a small, white-petaled flower.
When she would stumble
on this plant in the store
or the street
she'd announce in her tilted
accent "Ah Laaaaa"

with her nose buried deep
in green leaves as if
she had seen me that day
for the very first time.

Ibrik

I.

I found five Turkish coffee pots in the basement. This was after I
unbuttoned my sweater in several places. If I didn't move air closer
to my body, I would have buckled at the knees, felt cool cement
against my heart and cheek. I attend a funeral each day I spend
sorting through my mother's things. I worry I will only know her
as pots and pans, the ceramic bowls, and wedding China from
decades ago. Really, it's my hands I no longer recognize. They are
covered in dust and the thin translucent skins of bug shells and
body.

II.

These hands don't know how to heat an Ibrik on the stove.
It was my mother who prepared the coffee, poured dark rivers
into ceramic mouths, called my name to take a cup into the living
room. I never bothered to learn; never wanted to ask how she
boiled the coffee twice or held back sugar, so the coffee instead
tasted like layers of sediment deep underground, tasted like those
three languages knotted and turned on her tongue, tasted like the
basement's depth and the years stashed on shelves, tasted
like the dust in my hair
and my eyes.

Paper House

We live in a paper house.
That's what it feels like, anyway,
each day we discover
a new leak leaving damp circles
on the skin of crisp white paint
or find wood rotting at the roofline,
the back door, curled at the base
of a problem, simpering like skink
shadows on the porch—so
when we poke our fingers
into the places that should protect us,
wood flakes, falls—dandruff and scalp.
We live in a house of blind beliefs.
For example, we believe
the wood should not collapse
like it's tissue paper or bend
like it's a sponge. We believe the roof
shouldn't leak, and the old steel pipes
should never grow
red stalactites of rust.
For a long time, we believed
you weren't sick
when you outlined the shell
of this house, sketched it
in the air with your feet on the grass
and your eyes to the trees and sky.
We believed in the mathematical proof
that you had to live
if there was work set in motion—
each day they laid down tiles,
each evening with the click and slam
of planks for the hardwood floor,
bought a moment,
bought a minute,
bought the longer day.

We believed it was a good idea
at the time to buy the house
you never saw completed.
We believed we would make it whole.
There is no proof
that can measure the depth
of our disappointment.
There is no theorem
to bring you
home.

At the Souk

I.

I remember sitting on piles of Persian and Egyptian rugs. They were piled high as snow drifts, a height I knew well as a child of the snow.

We sat in the souk, two American-Egyptian kids, in the rug seller's place in the middle of Cairo, a city with borders that moved and flowed like the tentacles of an octopus, a city without stillness. My brother and I mountaineers atop silk and wool, our backs against the colors and swirls of our culture, dreaming we had touched the highest peaks and the sun through breaking clouds, bracing ourselves for the salesman's shout to get down from our heights— a shout in a language that runs on the page from right to left in elegant scrolls. A language we knew, oh we knew it, it was part of us, but it slipped by us like a chain in our hands, and we did not understand the words.

All this dreaming and running around and hiding from the salesman while you spent hours tracing colorful patterns with your eyes, your fingers touching the quality of the rugs, your mouth in that very strange language bargaining for the very best price.

You and dad would roll the rugs, fold them, and stuff them into empty suitcases, the bounty from your visit to your home country. They'd arrive on the baggage carousel in upstate New York with tape around their long, plump bodies, banged up and tired from travel.

They'd arrive, shocked and surprised, at landing in this new, strange, cold, foreign place.

II.

In the years after you died, I had to convince dad over many
months that I did not want the things you had carried so carefully
from far away. I watched him roll the rugs like handmade
cigarettes and movers took them away, piled them high in the
corners of a Midwest storage unit to be sold. I watched quietly.
Maybe you did, too, from somewhere far away.

I remembered where they came from and the journey they took. I
remember you and the way you chose these pieces of your country
so I may know where I came from each time I stepped into a room.
I remembered their weight, in the suitcase, on the baggage
carousel. I remembered all this as my eyes followed the truck
carrying this weight away from me, my heart free.

Notice You

I dug my fingers deep
in a mulch bed.
This was where I first
began to dream.
My mother would let
the sun dip low
before she called me in,
sent me straight to the sink
to wash dark matter
from my nails and hands
like I had scratched away
the sky on nights
I couldn't find the moon.
These are the parts of me
I notice when you run
out the front door
on the warmest winter day,
when you stand at the border
of mulch beds, circle
the trees with your arms.
I want to take you
by your shoulders, say
catch this now
catch this fast
get your clothes dirty
and dig up every worm.
I want to say
I miss the way my mother
looked at me
when the day was over
when water was boiling
in a roll on the stove
when time together started
when my hands were dry
and clean.

Cell Division & Other Science

My father—an electrical engineer—taught me to divide on my hands. It started when I asked what the sign with the bar and two dots meant. *Division,* he said, voice low, as if numbers were as divine as prayer. *What happens,* my father asked, *when you divide four by two?* He held my small hands in his, took four of my fingers gently split them into two pairs of two. I didn't understand not all numbers break this way, with a line down the middle clean and crisp like cracking ice. I spent the morning deciphering long division my father promised could be answered in the way my fingers bounced between their neighbors, rocking heavy as metal balls in Newton's cradle, steady as the spin of the earth. I thought of my hands the day my friend told me she'd had a hard time staying pregnant. Cells divide and grow until the calculus and the long division of new life are no longer possible for her to carry them. She doesn't cry, but I know she's asking for a new mathematical formula. She's plotting stars in the universe, charting new formations so the summation and negations make sense. I did the same those years ago when my mother's cells divided uncontrollably, two by two by two like soap bubbles slick and oily in the light. My hands knew the counts were off. I could snap my fingers at the knuckles to account for decimal points
and all the cells that broke the rules. But my hands are imperfect calculators for bodies that ache when it's cold and breathe in the face of a dying sun.

Grotto of Our Lady of Lourdes

A sonnet for G&E

We got lost on the way there. A cool wind
through the early evening—
a pending storm. In my hands
a campus map I pulled open in squares.
You wouldn't tell me where we were going,
enjoyed instead watching me wander gray
paths and green lawns in search of something while
our girl ran away in laughter. Ran wild.

We turned the corner. I felt the heat
before I saw the light. This is what prayer looks like.
A memory of my mother first.
Our daughter turned and asked *why is mommy crying?*
Before the answer, she took off running
unafraid of the coming storm, disrupting ducks asleep.

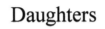
Daughters

Here

My daughter is the German-Polish border
that moved across Danzig. She's
the old stone castles of Irish fields.
My daughter is the city of Palmyra
before its columns were destroyed. She's
the white sands of the Sphinx. She's a mountain
in Beirut made of Cedar groves.
My daughter won't know Arabic in the way
I heard the language split French phrases
in my parents' house. She won't know the German
her father's forebears whispered
when the night would rock their ship
from sea to here.
My daughter's hair is soil in sun,
her skin an almond shell. Her eyes
are olive branches, her lashes shade.
My daughter laughs the way
the sky sounds just before it rains. She
cries in riverbeds where the rocks
have gone soft.
My daughter speaks.
When my daughter speaks
her voice is a wildflower planted

far from here.

Outer Space

You ask me difficult questions.
For example, five words circle your brain
like your body and blue scooter
circling the drive:

Mommy—
what's past outer space?

Past the blue band holding
us in and together; this must be
how stillness hangs at the boundaries,
where the wind blows sideways and
the tilted spider breaks the line it made
in the sky.

This is suspension; what
my parents felt when they left their country
for a frozen place. This is atmosphere,
what my grandparents breathed
when they left cedar mountains
for the Nile.

The countries of the Middle East
have no boundaries in my blood.
If I swab the lining of my mouth,
if I wrap my spit in a test tube,
and send it to a sterile lab,
I will have no better understanding
of my home.

You mark now two generations deep
in this country. Your English is not mixed
with other languages.
You have no conflict in your heart.

When you are older, I can't tell you
if your heritage will shake you
from the dead of your sleep,
from a deep night,
from a dream gone cold.

I can't tell you what you'll long for.
I long for the black birds my mother told me
are the real Egyptians, birds born
when the Pharaohs birthed language
and built wooden boats
with sails to catch the wind.

Daughter, I can tell you—
the first time you stand on sand
at the base of the Pyramids,
watch the Nile turn yellow
in the lights of a nighttime city,
you will float, astronaut untethered
between the planets
and the stars.

Silver-Plated

The summer my daughter turned five
she learned how to swim.
She took big breaths between breaks
in her stroke, her hands cupped the water
and legs kicked up white froth.
Each year she grows like a wildflower—taller.
Each year more words attach themselves
to her sentences, pulls her into a current
further from her heritage.

I know she won't know
the silver-sided leaves that grow
on bushes found on an island
in the Nile. My mother showed me
how to press the leaf in a heavy book
and in time, the silver would shine
like coins in the sun.

I cannot replicate my upbringing
for my little girl.
There is no cut and paste.
I don't speak my parents' language
or know the songs from over there.
I do not carry the recipes in my hands—
phyllo dough wrapped pastries,
rolled leaves (grape and cabbage),
kofta flat in its tray, cut in diagonal lines.
The smells that stay with my daughter
will not be the same ones
that have stayed with me.
Sumac. Cumin. Mint. Garlic.
I dream of these smells mixed
with my mother's scent.

I don't know the name
for the silver-sided leaf.
It grows sideways from bushes
bordering broken sidewalks
in a blistering Cairene sun.
When my mother took me on walks
through her old neighborhood,
she counted sightings by touch
of her favorite leaf.
You can only see the silver, she said
if you peel the green away,
bend it from the branch,
and press its body for years in a place
away from the sun.

Small Thing

I hold your face
in my hands. I want
a good look, every
fleck of gold and green
in your eyes. I'm searching
for all the small things
I've lost—loose change,
pencils, a quartz prism
on a chain my mother
gave me when I was young.

There was a time
I stood at the base
of the Great Pyramid
in Giza. The sand
in this part of the desert
is white and sometimes
yellow. I was your size then
and if I stretched my arms
wide against the limestone
my fingertips would never
know stone edges.

You're being patient, I know.
You're trying to keep still
while I search for myself
across the plateau of your skin.
How is it possible
your surfaces look like the shape
and color of limestone,
where the rock is smooth
and the sun is bright?

You've discovered, if you
listen closely, you can hear
the rain crack open stones
and your beating heart.
You dreamed a storm
had melted our house
in certain places,
and when your eye
found a hole in the roof
you saw a packet of light—
pretend moon hanging
from the sky
like a sand dollar suspended
in the sea.

You wiggle free
from my hands, stretch
your arms high to reach
my edges.
The doctors say
you'll be taller than me
one day.
I can't worry about
this yet, when
you'll grow into your feet,
when you'll grow out
of my help or my hugs, when
you'll fall out of my hands
like pea gravel between
my fingers, the kind
my mother would pocket
on a walk up
someone's driveway

and hand to us with joy
like she had found gold
in the street.

Telephone

Something told me to phone
my grandmother
tonight.

She answered and
her voice changed when
she heard my broken French across the line,
her voice warmed like spilled
ice cream on black pavement; ran
downhill into happy tears.
This is my own fault, I know,
for letting time run so long
without calling. Like sand through a sieve,
so careless and forgetful of me.

My mother used to tell me
her childhood stories of
Alexandria, where
tin cans tied by strings
tethered my grandmother
to neighbors across buildings
above the boardwalk
by the sea.
I thought of my voice through a tin can,
through a string above a city,
thought how much in this life
must have changed
in my grandmother's eyes.

I am aching in this hollow place
that has grown behind my heart.
It's the size of a home a squirrel
makes in the brush and
as wide as the Mediterranean Sea.

It's the length of a walk through
knee-high grasses and
as gray as a summer sky.

I ache because my daughter is growing,
and time is changing coastlines,
I ache because
nothing is the same, or
as I wanted it to be.
I ache for my grandmother's memories,
that I may know Alexandria
and her shorelines—
before years of storms
before the telephone
had come.

Feather

My uncle tells me
I'm the feather of the family.
I think about
what this means
and if I should fear the wind
or the birds who scavenge
lost feathers for their nests.
I heard once
feathers are stronger
than carbon fiber.
After all, feathers
are made of proteins resistant
to bacteria, to cuts
and bruises from the sky.
Water beads doesn't it,
on the back of a bird
when it rains?
I know that when
my uncle pulled this word
through his teeth
it had come packaged
in another language.
His mind said one thing,
his English gave me
feather.
It is possible
in his native tongue
I am not really a feather
but something else—
I am hopeful
it all means the same,
and when trouble comes,
I float.

Epilogue: Memory

Little Things

Something about Los Angeles
reminds me of Cairo.
In the taxi the world pulls away from me
like I have vertigo
or had too much to drink.
I take note of all the little things
I knew once, twenty years ago
about a city in the desert,
or the one by the sea—
the power lines that hang like hammocks
between the low buildings
hugging the rim of the city
like a child at her mother's knees.
Little things like the pale pink and yellow
hues of cracked plaster
and hand-painted signs.
The scent of gasoline like a spice
in the air. The palm trees.

The palm trees bleeding
through a haze when dusk
smudges the sky.
Is it strange a palm tree here
looks like a palm tree there
and when they bend
like a bridge toward the sun
never seem to want the rain?

About the Author

Yasmin Mariam Kloth writes creative nonfiction and poetry. Her writing, often rooted in her Middle Eastern heritage, scratches at love, loss, place, and space. Her work has appeared in *JuxtaProse, Cathexis Northwest Press, Chestnut Review, All the Sins, Kairos Literary Review,* the *Rockvale Review,* and others. Yasmin lives in Cincinnati, Ohio, with her husband and daughter. *Ancestry Unfinished* is her first published collection of poetry.